THERE ONCE WAS A BOBBY

THERE ONCE WAS A BOBBY

W. Andrew

Book Guild Publishing
Sussex, England

920. ANDL

First published in Great Britain in 2005 by
The Book Guild Ltd
25 High Street
Lewes, East Sussex
BN7 2LU

Typesetting in Times by
Acorn Bookwork Ltd, Salisbury, Wiltshire

Printed in Great Britain by
CPI Bath

A catalogue record for this book is available from
The British Library.

ISBN 1 85776 901 5

1

'I will get that bugger Lewis if it's the last thing I do before I retire.'

Lewis owned several two-up two-down terraced houses, mostly Victorian, in the old cutlery-manufacturing area of Sheffield. This was before the advent of industrial estates and before Hitler redesigned the architecture of this wonderful old city – for ever.

Due to the concentration of steel works, Sheffield received the third highest tonnage of bombs dropped by the Germans on Britain. Many of the inhabitants of these lowly properties were women, pensioners and children. Nearly every man of serviceable age was away fighting. The majority of these men were cutlers and not officially graded as essential steel workers and therefore not exempt from call-up. Without a breadwinner in the house, the lack of home garden produce and wartime rationing, their usually low standard of living was drastically reduced and being bombed out, sometimes more than once, only made things worse. Despite their deprivation, it was essential that the weekly rent took priority.

Lewis not only expected but demanded prompt payment. It was sometimes inevitable, especially during the harsh winter months, that funds for heat and food were scarce, so unfortunately the rent money was hard to find. He was not a charitable person, he would effect one of three courses of action: eviction, offers of a loan at exorbitant rates of interest or seizure of assets such as family heirlooms, pocket watches, jewellery etc. It was also rumoured that he was sometimes paid 'in kind' by the desperate women of the house.

There had been a fall of snow one night early in the first winter of the 'Blitz' and the next morning, being Friday, found him doing his usual door to door rent collection. On these visits he always travelled in his large Rover saloon car. This was the source of the conflict between him and the local police and in particular one certain police constable – the subject of this story. His concern was, where did Lewis obtain his petrol? This was a large greedy car and the meagre fuel allowance for essential use was certainly not adequate for the blatant prolific cruising around the local countryside with his 'Good Lady'. She was a corpulent lady with a distinctive style of dress which included a fur shawl around her neck – it was the body of a real animal – head, teeth, legs and claws, a macabre item.

The Lewises had a large house and estate several miles away from these rented properties, a trip Lewis performed regularly – his petrol consumption was obviously immense. On this particular snowy day an irate Lewis telephoned the police house.

He spluttered, 'Some urchin has thrown a snowball at me and knocked my expensive bowler hat from my head into the snow. It is ruined. It is an assault and I demand you come down here immediately and apprehend the culprit. I recognise him, he lives in one of my houses – not much longer if I can help it. He should show more respect and gratitude to his betters.'

As well as snow there had been some heavy bombing during the night. A public house had suffered a direct hit, there were many casualties and there were bodies everywhere. Most of the unfortunates had died of shock. The rescue workers had dragged them from the ruins and placed them in a sitting position against a wall opposite

the pub. They looked as if they were sleeping – it was a haunting sight. The police and fire brigade were badly stretched and as was usual on these occasions, police from the lesser damaged suburbs came in to help.

As the incumbent village bobby living in the police house on the outskirts, he was summoned by Lewis to attend this incident, which he did. It was on his way to help out at the Blitz site. He had been up all night on duty and was not in any mood to spend too much time on sympathy for Lewis. This may provide the opportunity to discover where Lewis obtained his petrol – a trivial ambition when measured against the necessity to assist in the disaster only a mile away. However, he was well aware Lewis had some discreet association with the Superintendent and it was not wise to ignore his demand.

A crowd of about 20 women and children surrounded the Rover. A terrified Lewis cowered inside – evidence of the snowball missiles was everywhere, there were even some inside the car. This had occurred when he had left it to dash to a nearby telephone box. They were a frightening group, they screeched and yelled excitedly – this abated somewhat on the arrival of the policeman.

'He's asked for it,' shouted a scrawny unkempt young mother nursing a sleeping plump baby. 'He's threatened to evict our Mary and her family and the poor girl's husband is missing, somewhere in France. She has offered to pay him all the money she has, about half of his rent. Can't you do something to help, Officer? Please.'

Lewis wound down his window.

'Thank goodness you have finally arrived, Officer. Control them, they are like savages – I hold you personally responsible if anything happens to me, or the Rover.'

'Will you please pass me the keys, sir?' said the PC.

'No, I will not,' replied Lewis. 'Why do you need them?'

'I wish to look inside the boot, Mr Lewis.'

Lewis reluctantly passed the keys. He opened the boot expecting to find a petrol can with markings which may provide a clue to its origin. He was disappointed. No such luck. However, there were two large wooden crates, each containing a gross of oranges.

Lewis almost screamed, 'Keep out of there, it's private.'

The officer beckoned to two of the older boys about 12 years of age.

'Take the oranges and distribute them to everyone here – and then all of you go home.'

The oranges vanished as if by magic – all except two of them. These were enjoyed by my sister and myself – it was the first time we had tasted such fruit.

'You are stealing my property. They are valuable, I paid a lot for them – I shall report you, Constable. How can you as a custodian of the law sanction such an irresponsible action?'

He stared at Lewis for a few seconds and then he said quietly, 'Believe me, sir, I have no animosity against you or your race, in fact I have a great deal of sympathy for your people, but please be mindful of the fact that most of these women's husbands are away fighting to protect you from the evil forces against you, many of them will not return – it is you who should be grateful to them. Report me, by all means, sir. You must now tell me where you obtained the oranges, you can include that in your report.'

Lewis did not pursue the matter further – however he did report the policeman for anti-Semitic remarks made before witnesses. It was not likely that any witnesses would have been forthcoming. He did receive an official reprimand, the only one in an otherwise exemplary career, which also included three commendations.

I have selected this incident to illustrate the character

of a very conscientious police officer. He was not always politically correct – not always gentle with bullies or violent men, but I can vouch for the fact that as his son, who I admit often deserved punishment, he never once smacked me. My mother, now 96 and still living in the same police house, just seven stone and half his size, terrorised him.

This incident occurred mid career, he did eventually 'get Lewis' for obtaining black market petrol.

2

Born on the outskirts of Nottingham in 1904, he had three brothers and a sister, one of his brothers being his identical twin, almost impossible to tell them apart – except in spirit.

His father, my grandfather worked on the railway for 54 years – not missing a single day's service, except for the period between the first day of the war in 1914 until the last day of hostilities in 1918. Most of these years were spent in France and according to him usually up to his neck in mud. He hardly ever mentioned his experiences. Most of his colleagues were killed early on. Strangely enough, in later years he always mentioned the German soldiers with respect and grudging admiration. He returned to his family unannounced the day after the war ended without so much as a scratch – he proudly presented two kitbags full of tins of butter, two large brass fieldgun shell cases, large enough to be used as umbrella holders, and a German silver-cased pocket watch and chain – which I now own. He said that when

he found it buried in the mud it was filthy. He carefully cleaned it and the bloke it belonged to had no further use for it. Some 20 years later I learned to tell the time with this watch. His advice to me when I was called up for National Service in the RAF was – learn to say 'Sir' to a pig, keep your feet dry and keep your hand on your halfpenny in the ablutions. I was never too sure what he meant by this.

I visited him in hospital just before he died – he had been poisoned by some contaminated freshwater crayfish he had taken from a gravel pit near the Trent. Turned 90 and obviously on his way out, he hung on for almost a week, insisting that he was not going until *he* was ready.

He entered the army as a regular Church of England worshipper and emerged as an atheist – however, he seemed concerned about the fact that in 1915 he had skewered two German soldiers on his bayonet at the same time.

'Do you think they will be waiting for me?'

My grandfather's experiences in the war did, however, leave their mark. He was disappointed when my father enlisted in the Regular Army as soon as he was old enough. He joined the Second Battalion Scots Guards and after completing his basic training he was stationed in Chelsea and served two years on guard duty at Buckingham Palace and the Bank of England. He became a fervent royalist a great admirer of the Prince of Wales. He was very impressed with how he treated the soldiers. He would visit them on duty and give them cigarettes and talk with them. The Abdication disappointed him, but not nearly as much as the recent revelations regarding his behaviour during the Second World War would have done.

He was posted from London to China and served there for four years. This was after the Boxer Rebellion and

was in support of the new regime under General Chang Chai Chek. He matured in China and enjoyed his sporting experiences where he boxed and played football for the British Army and also specialised in long-distance swimming.

There was a large Japanese presence at this time, mostly made up of visiting sailors, and he spoke of the constant conflict between themselves and the Japanese and less about the controlling of the rebels.

He put great faith in the prediction of a Chinese soothsayer whom he visited to have a troublesome corn removed from his foot. Although several army medics had attempted to remove it without success – the soothsayer did it immediately. The sage informed him that he would return to his homeland safely, enjoy a happy fruitful marriage and survive a long dangerous war when he would encounter many dangers. He must face these dangers, not to flinch and he would survive. It was also foreseen that he would die at the age of 72.

All this experience would prepare him mentally and physically for this future career when demobilised. These predictions were mostly proven correct. However, I can remember his seventy-first year was not a comfortable year. I am pleased to say this prediction was more than a decade out.

He immediately joined the Derbyshire County Police Force on leaving the Scots Guards and his first posting was as a PC in a mining community on the Nottingham – Derbyshire border. It was a harsh inauguration. His main duty involved him with the control of drunken mine workers, usually after pay day at the weekend.

He was invited to play football for one of the mine teams and I suspect it was the intention of players on both sides to take retribution for his policing duties. He said that for three months his legs were black and blue with bruises, but he probably gave as good as he got.

3

One of the incidents he recalled from his first posting was very macabre. The Derby to Nottingham LMS railway line passed through the town where there were large lakes created by the indiscriminate mining of open-cast coal. One of the larger lakes was adjacent to the main line. Suicides are not a twenty-first century phenomena. They were very common during these depressed times.

The point where the line came closest to the lake was known locally as 'suicide corner'. They either jumped into the lake, or lay across the lines. One dark night his

sergeant took him to his incident where an adult male had chosen the line rather than the water. His instructions were to collect the scattered body parts necessary for the inquest. The railway police would be responsible for the trunk, for which they had a stretcher, he would locate and recover the head and take it to the ambulance.

The sergeant, a sensitive soul, believed in on-the-job training and imparted to him what he considered to be a valuable tip.

He said, 'When you find his head, carry it at arm's length and hold it by the hair and it won't spoil your uniform.'

To his dismay, the man was completely bald. Determined to impress his superior, he sought him out in the darkness and informed him of the problem.

'What shall I do, Sarge?' he enquired.

The sergeant sighed.

'Do I have to tell you everything – use his bloody ears.'

He served in this community for just over two years when he was called to the headquarters in Derby.

4

Percy Sillitoe had been given the unenviable task of cleaning up the gangs in Sheffield. They were terrorising the city. The situation was becoming intolerable and out of hand. Locals were fearful of walking the streets at night. He invited unmarried constables over six feet in height and over 14 stones in weight to be recruited to a newly-formed gang busting squad. They would be offered free lodgings – but no extra pay. He applied and was accepted. This is how he came to live in the area.

Lodgings were found in the home of another policeman and his family. The house unchanged today, is still bleak and in a very windy situation on the edge of the Derbyshire moors to the south-west of Sheffield. There were two secure cells under the house which were used for temporary custody – usually drunks or poachers.

Their brief from the Chief Constable was to do whatever to keep the peace. They would get his full support just so long as he did not have to sign a Coroner's report. The man in charge, now Sir Percy Sillitoe, published his autobiography many years later giving great detail.

The strategy was to visit a public house frequented by gang members, to be alone and dressed in plain clothes. He would order a pint and engage the landlord in conversation. Gradually he would bad-mouth members of the Mooney or Garrety gang by name. Suitably baited, some of the thugs would move menacingly towards him. At the last moment he would blow his whistle and many of his colleagues would appear from nowhere and a violent affray would ensue.

He appeared to almost enjoy these skirmishes especially as he was on the right side of the law. He used to say it was almost as difficult as it had been in Hong Kong in the 1920s when six Guardsmen were expected to clear a bar of 20 Japanese sailors. These seamen were very cruel to the Chinese natives who were considered to be inferior to them and who were in fact terrorised by them. Even then he felt he was on the right side of the law. Eventually the gangs were controlled and the young policemen returned to their own local force. He remained in this area and transferred to the City of Sheffield Police.

It was shortly after this he married and moved into a new house in the same area – this became the local police house. I was born in this house almost 70 years ago, my mother still lives there. I noticed on my last visit eight small holes in the brickwork and from old photographs was able to identify that four of them were for fixing the Derbyshire County Police Emblem – the other four for the Sheffield City Police badge.

My sister, three years younger than myself, was born in the same bed in the same room – I was born in Derbyshire, she in Yorkshire.

As the village 'bobby' in the 30s before the Second World War, life was very bucolic, his duties mainly involving poaching, domestic disturbance and the odd house breaking – the latter he was convinced were perpetrated by 'Sheffielders' straying into the village. Some Sunday lunchtimes he would position himself at the bus terminus on the edge of the village and if they looked suspicious he would escort them back on to the bus and return them back to where they came from. Coming up here leaving empty 'pop' bottles to damage the livestock and they even push wall tops off he would say. When the war started he maintained that if they had sent a group of these Sheffield hooligans to Germany they would have terrified the Germans and war would have been avoided!

One of the first memories he could recall from childhood was an event which occurred before the First World War was officially declared.

Some German aviators in a balloon had dropped bricks, one of them killing the Co-op dray horse and his father said to him, 'This is going to be a dirty war, there will be no place for honourable warriors any more.'

Earlier in the year I accompanied my elder son on a visit to my mother and took the opportunity to conduct him on a tour of the village he had left as a small child and I thought it would familiarise him with some of the locations and more memorable features he had only previously heard about. We had a pint in the local pub which had probably changed little from when it had been

the central point of his grandfather's beat. I indicated some brickwork of about two square feet which did not match the surrounding surface. This had been a serving hatch where locals would take a jug to be filled with draught beer without needing to enter the building. It was a halfpenny a pint cheaper. It was also the exact spot where he would visit halfway through his night shift and pick up a pint left there by the landlady. He was enjoying such a pint one frosty night when he noticed the duty sergeant walking towards him. He held the half-full tankard under his police cape as they discussed the night's events. Discipline was much more rigid at this time and he was fearful his superior would smell beer on his breath. Eventually after about ten minutes the sergeant bade him goodnight and set off to inspect the constable on the next area beat.

As he turned to go he said, 'Don't finish that pint until I am well out of sight or I will have to report you if I see you.'

At the brow of the hill not far from this point there is another peculiar feature of the area I thought my son would be interested to see. At the end of the 1920s and up to the war it was common for men to compete in the 100 yard dash and the measured mile for money prizes, the Powderhall chase being an example. Unofficial betting was popular and large amounts of money could be won. This made the competitors technically professionals and debarred them from amateur events and of course the Olympic Games. Some of the young men were accomplished athletes, their times being not far from Olympic standards. Often those who were known to have accepted money went on to play Rugby League. Rugby Union was strictly amateur and forbidden to them. A well-known local lad was showing signs of great promise as a sprinter and his father was encouraging him to turn pro.

My father enquired his time and on being told it was over 10.5 seconds, said, 'He will never make it, some of the league players do even time in rugby boots,' probably an exaggeration.

He said to the boy's father, 'I will bet you a pint of best that I can beat him over 80 yards. I am not as fit as I was in the army or I would challenge him to the hundred. Providing no one sees us, I pick the track and all I ask for is one yard start as a handicap. This offer is fair and if he is as good as you claim and in full training it will be a useful experience for him.'

The boy's father, proud and confident of his son's ability, shook hands with him – the deal was on. The following night they met as agreed at the rear of the pub, both in vests, shorts and running shoes. My father led the way to the selected track, across the road, up a few steps and through a gateway in a high stone wall. They entered a passageway exactly one yard wide, 80 yards in length. Between the two high walls it was impossible to overtake. The lad never became a professional, but he had a very successful amateur career.

5

It was around this time I was born. One of my earliest lessons from him was in the selection of hens' eggs. He would take me with him to the fishmonger's shop in the village – usually on a Saturday morning before the match. This was before restrictions on uniform sizing, date stamps, etc. They were all free range from a local farm. A huge basket was filled with the eggs of varying colours and sizes. The fishmonger would place either six or twelve eggs in a box, the price always the same.

My father knew him well and they would discuss the team's prospects and the danger of a war starting soon and he would help himself to the eggs at the same time. He took his time since it was his practice only to select eggs laid by a brown hen. Not the colour of the egg – but the colour of the bird, Rhode Island Reds being his favourite. It was a ritual. He would occasionally hold the egg up to the sun before placing it in the box. The fishmonger was always suitably puzzled. He admitted he himself was unable to identify them. Eventually satisfied, they were all from brown hens he would pay up and leave the mystified shopkeeper scratching his head in disbelief and marvelling at his supernatural powers.

When the war eventually commenced food was rationed, including eggs, so already almost self-sufficient for produce from his vegetable garden and his allotment, he decided to raise hens. He built a chicken coop from heavy timber, his only tools being a hammer, a wood saw and a carving knife. The saw he borrowed from the man next door. He was not a gifted DIY person but after several days of cursing, struggling and swearing, a very stout construction was completed. It still stands today after the Blitz and 60 years of northern winters.

He bought twelve hens at the point of lay and two cockerels. Throughout the war and many years after we enjoyed fresh eggs daily and a roasted cockerel for Christmas dinner always named Hector and the other for New Year's Day. He was called Horace. They were replaced in January. The hens were usually brown but their numbers were made up by a few black or white hens.

One year when buying new stock I enquired, 'Why if you prefer brown hens' eggs do you include black and white birds?'

He looked rather surprised at my stupidity. He admitted it was impossible to tell which bird the eggs came from. He just carefully selected the 12 biggest eggs. Recently I passed this knowledge on to my granddaughter. She is fortunate in living in a village where unsorted fresh farm eggs are available.

At quite an early age I realised I could disappoint him. He would really have liked me to be better at football than I looked like being. I would never reach his standard. He had played for the army and occasionally with Notts County when on leave. I loved to play and eventually obtained a place in the school team but I was very relieved when a friend introduced me to the Sheffield Tigers Rugby Club. It was generally accepted then and to some extent still is, that boys who are not talented enough to play good soccer go to play rugby and those who can do neither go to play tennis with the girls. We of course all played cricket.

I played five seasons with the club and two for the squadron when in the RAF – he only ever came to see me play once. It was a Christmas fixture against Leeds – the only time I was ever sent off. Neither of us ever mentioned the incident.

Gradually his support for Notts County waned and he became a member of the Sheffield United Football Club.

On the day of a home match at Bramall Lane he came across little Jimmy, a part-time employee of the local newspaper – part-time street hawker. 'Im-n-er (him & her), Im-n-er you can't have him without her. Sixpence for the two of them.' He had a large pile of black and white photos of him and a similar quantity of her. They had been copied probably illegally and stolen from the print room of the newspaper.

He was the Prince of Wales and very desirable and popular. *She* was Mrs Wallace Simpson, neither desirable nor popular. 'Hark the Herald Angels sing, Mrs Simpson's pinched out King.' To make a profit Jimmy must sell both photos. They must be purchased as a pair.

My father was a strong supporter of Royalty and

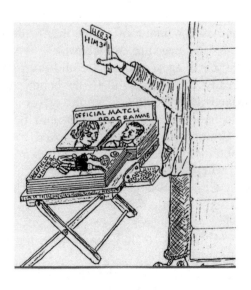

admired 'David', hoping one day he would be king. Sometimes on Sunday evenings when in the company of my aunt and uncle he would draw the curtains, lower his voice almost to a whisper and tell stories of life at the Palace which he had observed first hand when on guard duty there. He would recount tales of lurid experiences and liaisons between Royal females and guardsmen. A particular young lady would request the services of a particular soldier usually on Friday evenings and of course when he was on duty there. The guardsman, in the same billet as my father, was very loyal and reasonably discreet and swore his colleagues to secrecy, just as my aunt and uncle were many years later when after the Abdication my father thought it 'safe to tell'. Now, looking back on these tales, I realise the antics of the current incumbents of the Palace are merely keeping up the tradition.

It saddened and annoyed him to hear little Jimmy making a profit from selling photographs of her.

'Have you got a licence for selling on this pitch, Jimmy?' he asked, knowing full well he had not. 'If you sell any more I will nick you.'

Jimmy looked pathetic.

'Have a heart, Bobby, I need to get rid of all of these as soon as possible so that I can get to the match before kick-off.'

He, like my father, was a keen supporter of the 'Blades'. A compromise was reached.

'You can carry on, Jimmy, if you only sell the photos of the Prince.'

It was agreed

'Thanks, Bobby. I hope we beat Newcastle his afternoon'.

As he walked away he heard Jimmy cry, 'Im alone only sixpence, Im alone.'

6

I remember his identical twin brother John, known as
Jack. I only ever saw him once, at my grandfather's
funeral – and then never again.

It was the first time my father had met him in over 30
years. As they stood together at the graveside they were
still absolutely identical and, strangely, they wore the
same suits and shoes. It was difficult to understand how
they had become so estranged living only 28 miles apart.
Their separation was self-imposed and occurred as the
result of a most silly incident.

The police house I described has an indoor toilet (one
of the first in the area) to the left at the top of the stairs.
Whenever I use this toilet I am reminded with amazement
of what had occurred on this very spot. My Uncle John
married Aunt Gladys at about the same time as my
mother and father married. They were 'best man' at each
other's wedding. Gladys and my mother were brides-
maids at each other's wedding.

Gladys, a pretty, dainty girl, was a fervent Baptist and
was working on John to become the same. Welsh in
origin and ultra-puritanical, she terrorised him, forbade
him to touch alcohol or to fraternise with those who did,
this included his father and his brothers, and gradually
she won him over. Shortly after their marriage she
overheard him say 'Damn' and refused to speak to him
for a week.

My parents invited them to visit them for a week's
holiday – they had been warned they were teetotal, even

my mother was informed of the ill effects of her daily sherry – a weakness she indulges some 70 years on. My father visited this toilet and not being used to having other people in the house he neglected to close the toilet door. He was standing facing the toilet with his back to the doorway when a small hand slid between his legs and tickled his scrotum. There was a girlish giggle and a little voice said, 'Tinkle, tinkle.'

My father, expecting it to be my mother, turned around and to their mutual embarrassment saw it was Gladys. She insisted they packed their bags immediately and leave the house to catch the next train – which they did. There was no communication between the twin brothers for over 30 years. My father made several attempts to remedy the situation, particularly at Christmas, but without success. He would receive a card signed John, probably sent in secret. My mother was relieved to be able to continue with her sherry but the brothers had enjoyed their last beer together.

7

The objective of this writing is to illustrate the life and character of this particular policeman. The events are not in chronological order but have been selected to make a point at the relevant time.

Although reprimanded as a racist, he would have needed to enquire the meaning of the word. He most certainly was not. Not so Mr Parry, Mr Ted Parry – dentist, a strict man in his fifties, married, childless and a pillar of the local Parish Church. I was always wary of him, never more than when tempted by his apple tree – the bearer of the best fruit in the village. Although the tree overhung the public field to the rear of the house, windfalls were available to all, but the better ones were at the other side of the wall. Once caught at the illicit side of the wall by an understandably irate Mr Parry, there was little evidence of his Lord's edict regarding suffering little children. To be fair to him though, he did not report me to my father.

He was a keen cricket fan and a member of the Yorkshire County Cricket Club. In later years I came to respect him especially for his patient tuition when he helped me to bowl leg breaks.

Before the mass immigration of the Asians to Sheffield, a few West Indians were encouraged to come and live and work in the city, especially if they possessed some of the scarce required skills. Many local men had been lost in the war and during the post-war boom time there was a severe labour shortage. They were eagerly accepted to drive buses, trams and taxis and to work in hospitals and engineering factories – not so much in the steel works. Subsidised Council housing was arranged for them. Generally this scheme worked well as it encouraged integration, a benefit Sheffield enjoys currently. Although there has been a large number of people coming into the City, there are very few racism problems.

Although geographically Yorkshire, Sheffielders are not the stereotypical harsh northerners; they are very tolerant people. Mr Parry was an exception. He called at the police house in a very irate mood, complaining that a 'Black Family' had been billeted in the now vacant doctor's house next door to him. He protested that they were noisy and the smell of their cooking was not acceptable in his crescent. This had all the signs of a disturbance. He went to investigate. The West Indian, a tall, well-built young man opened the door to him. His wife, a pretty, heavily pregnant young lady, cowered timidly behind him. Mr Parry appeared from nowhere.

'You can see for yourself, Constable, they are not suitable people for our neighbourhood.'

Joe, the angry newcomer looked menacingly at the officer and said, 'I see you two are friends. I will not expect any justice from you. We have done no harm and he has frightened my wife. If he does not go away he will regret it.'

'Behave yourself, Joe – and listen to me.' He turned to Mr Parry and said, 'You should be ashamed of yourself, Ted. Is it not in your creed that you should love your neighbour as yourself? What sort of example do you think you are setting to the newcomers. You should invite Joe and his wife to your church. Although I feel more like knocking your heads together for wasting police time, I will be satisfied with a handshake and two promises. From you, Ted, invite them to your church, I know they are of the same faith as yourself and Mrs Perry.' He then turned to Joe's wife. 'Mrs Jaques, when that child of yours is born, if it's a boy – please put his name down to play cricket for Yorkshire – I know a good coach.'

She nodded and smiled shyly – the men shook hands and although it would be exaggerating to claim they became blood brothers they actually became good neighbours.

My mother asked him how he knew of the Jaques' faith being the same as Mr Parry's.

He said, 'Being a policeman gives you a special understanding of spiritual matters – besides I saw the Bible on the hall table.'

8

Men employed in the steel industry were exempt from call-up for military service – this did them no favours as they worked day and night with little time off and all the time being a prime target for the Luftwaffe. Most of them were hard, heavy drinking characters and as never before had the country depending upon them.

Two of the more notorious residents on his beat were the Reilly brothers. Although hardworking and very patriotic, they had a streak of Robin Hood in their character.

It was a hot Sunday afternoon, their first break in ten days and their first time in the open air. They were selling 'bits of mutton' from the back of an old red van. The van was parked on a corner just visible from the main road. He walked over to investigate. The brothers were so engrossed in their distribution of the assumed illicit meat that they did not see him approach. The first sign of anything unusual was when an excited woman in hair curlers wearing a flowered apron flecked with blood spots ran past him with the front leg and neck of a sheep under her arm. It was still half covered with skin and wool. She had bought it for sixpence. There was sufficient meat to feed her family for several days.

Although the brothers were skilled steel workers, they were very inadequate butchers. There were still two live sheep in the back of the van and the bloody remains of probably two others scattered around their feet. The happy customers had not seen so much meat since it went on ration at the beginning of the war. They were taking full advantage and grabbing all they could.

On seeing him approach, Pete the younger brother said, 'It's all legal, officer, these animals strayed into our back garden and were fritting the missus. The law says we won them.'

He looked at the policeman hopefully. There were no grazing sheep to be found within several miles of this part of the city. He surmised that they had been rustled from the Chatsworth estate. After waiting a few minutes until the remains of the sheep were gathered up, he instructed them to secure the two live sheep in the van and give him the ignition key. He put the brothers in the rear of the police car along with a fleece. The fleece was to be used in evidence. He asked them to empty their pockets. There was less than two pounds, all in bloodied copper coins. After counting the money he put it in a pouch and wrote the amount on the outside of an envelope which he then sealed carefully. He then commenced to take them to the police station to charge them.

Petrol was scarce even for official journeys and after about half a mile the car spluttered to a halt – he had run out of petrol. Still about half a mile from the station, he instructed them to get out and push all the way up the hill. This they did without complaint. Afterwards he was asked if they might abscond, he said it was not likely – he knew who they were, where they lived and where they worked and they would certainly not miss a shift, so the risk was minimal. However, just to make sure he had handcuffed them together and removed their shoes.

It was a difficult case – the brothers had not done it for financial gain the bloody money in the envelope hardly covered the cost of the petrol and they had made a lot of disadvantaged people happy, but the law had been broken.

His mind turned to his childhood when his father would produce their dinner from under his railway uniform top coat – usually a plump young wild rabbit. It always worried my grandmother, a very law-abiding lady, as poaching was considered to be quite a serious offence. His claim was always the same – he had exchanged it with a game keeper for a bucket of coal from the engine. He would raise the still warm rabbit and blow gently into its soft underbelly fur and then return it to the table.

'I always examine them, and the first time I see one with the Duke of Portland's name on it, I promise you I will return it.'

The sheep had no markings – they had not been reported stolen – so he made a decision.

'If you promise to deliver the two live sheep safely to where you found them the incident will not be recorded.

31

I will not tell your father – but it will not be forgotten.'

Not all his cases were so relatively harmless or concluded so satisfactorily. Sometimes they were quite harrowing, especially where children were concerned.

He visited a 'bombing out' where an incendiary bomb had burnt down two terrace cottages. Fortunately the families had managed to evacuate the damaged houses without injury – although their homes of many years had been destroyed. They had been asleep and fled to a neighbour's home about 200 yards away. They sheltered under blankets. The children were naked and shivering with shock and cold and their neighbours were desperately trying to find clothing for them.

When he returned home later than usual he persuaded my mother to hurry and make a warm skirt for a girl of about eleven years of age – he held his hand about three foot six from the ground, 'About this height'. He gave her his old guard's uniform tartan kilt – it was his most prized possession – she cut it down to size and made a passable garment for the unfortunate child. To finish it

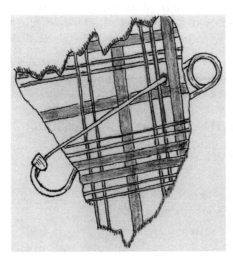

off he gave her the large steel kilt pin he had been issued with.

The next morning he took the garment to the grateful family who were now billeted with a cousin in the next street. It fitted the little girl perfectly and she was thrilled with it.

Just two nights later he came home distraught and angry. He put his hand in his pocket and brought out the kilt pin. I saw my mother cry – which was most unusual for her – when he whispered something to her. Later I was told the family had all been killed along with seven other relatives by a direct hit. He had attempted to save them from the ruins, along with the fire brigade – all he located was a small piece of charred tartan cloth and the kilt pin. I still possess this pin.

9

A car horn sounded in the street outside, I glanced through the window to see his small Morris Eight pass by. Unusually he did not stop. Then I noticed two soldiers sitting in the back seats holding a large object wrapped in an army blanket on their knees. He was driving.

They were taking an unexploded bomb which had fallen through the roof of the Midland Railway Station in the centre of the city to a safe place. It had rolled onto the platform and finally bounced onto the main Sheffield – London track. This was a busy line and the major communication between the two cities. The station was cleared and the line was closed. If the disposal squad were to explode it in situ lives would not be at risk but untold devastation to the station would be unacceptable. It would be difficult to estimate for how long the main line would be out of commission.

Two members of the disposal unit examined the bomb and took a calculated risk in suggesting it should be taken to a safe place. His advice for such a location was sought and he suggested an old disused ganister mine several miles distant on the moors. They wrapped it in a blanket and sat with it in the car and since he knew the site he drove. They duly exploded the bomb, which made a huge crater. Afterwards he was full of admiration for the two young soldiers.

He said, 'I hid behind a wall whilst they buggered about with it – I've never seen such brave men.'

I knew him well. He fully understood his own danger whilst driving the bomb in the car but he would never admit it.

This story involves another tangible momento of these times. Along with the kilt pin there is a piece of shrapnel from the bomb, about the size of a beer mug. It was still warm when he gave it to me.

It was roughly in this area that the paratroop regiment had trained for a special offensive. Probably about 2,000 volunteers were encamped in this moorland area. They did practice drops and each one of them had a small foldable motor scooter – Corgi – which they fastened to their backpack when not in use. It was a strange sight to see them riding in close formation along the road outside school and we would rush to the wall to wave to them. One Sunday lunchtime my father returned from the pub with two of these young men in uniform, Ken and Bill, both from Bromley in Kent. Mother fed them and they played with my sister and myself – Ken gave me a badge from his beret, the winged parachute, I wore it on my school blazer for years. They would visit us probably two evenings each week and bring tins of corned beef and bottles of beer as gifts. I became very fond of them. They obviously missed their own families.

As if by magic they disappeared overnight – the entire camp had vanished without trace. They had prepared to drop at Arnhem. The Germans had been forewarned and they shot them as they floated to the ground. Both were killed. We received a letter of thanks, giving us this information from one of their mothers, Ken's mother I think. She also said that her son had described the food my mother had given them especially the home-made bread.

He had said 'It's not bread it's better than bloody cake!'

10

Many of the incidents I remember vividly, especially those I witnessed personally. Some remain as brief fragments which come to life when I am reminded of similar incidents related more recently by someone who has shared the same experience.

It still comes as a shock to me when I hear such a story, as I did recently on the radio. Earlier I described the location of the police house situated on the Derbyshire-Yorkshire border. The nearby lake, originally used as a pond for providing water power for a wire mill, is subjected to the same boundary division – half in Derbyshire, half in Yorkshire.

He was instructed by his sergeant how to punt a floating suicide body from one county to the next. He had secreted a long pole under some bushes for this purpose. Apparently even in those days, 70 years ago, a considerable amount of time and effort on the necessary paperwork was avoided, affording him a free Saturday afternoon to see Sheffield United.

One particular Saturday afternoon United were playing Wednesday in a local derby at Bramall Lane. At this time they were both powerful clubs in the first division. By chance Derby County reserves were playing Wednesday reserves at Hilsborough at the other side of the city. It was lunchtime, he was on traffic control duty at a busy junction about halfway between the Police Station and Bramall Lane. With only an hour or so before kick-off he was required to return to the station to book off and relieve the afternoon shift. He was contemplating the possibility of getting to the match before half-time and not concentrating too diligently on the job in hand. His attention was alerted to the noise made by a car hooter being sounded repeatedly. He looked across the road and noticed a man was beckoning to him through the open window of a car. Waiting for the first opportunity to leave his point, it was a few minutes before he was able to walk over to the stationary vehicle.

The driver was furious and was displaying his temper to all around. His wife sat nervously by his side. He wore a black shirt, black shorts and football boots – he also had a silver chain around his neck from which dangled a silver whistle.

'Are you stupid, Constable, or just deaf? Did you not

hear me hoot you? I cannot tolerate such indiscipline. You will obey me immediately next time I come across you. I don't normally expect to have to tell anyone something twice – my wife here will vouch for that.' She nodded. 'A person of my status and importance cannot tolerate such idleness. I am the referee for the Derby match, the kick-off is at 2.45 p.m. and we are lost. The signposts in this city are hopeless, I will report your council to the AA tomorrow.'

As in most cities, signposts had been removed during the war and were rather late in being replaced.

'Very sorry, sir. I will tell you the best way and save you a few miles and some valuable time,' said the policeman helpfully.

He then carefully directed him to the Derby reserve match at Hilsborough, an understandable mistake. He had obeyed his instructions. He saluted the referee again, repeated his apology and set off for the police station.

The war obviously created much more pressure on the police. There was also a severe shortage of officers as many were killed or injured in the Blitz. Some had joined up, although this had not been obligatory, and the extra long working hours were taking their toll.

Many German aircraft were shot down during their raids on the city, which also increased the burden on the police since any of the crew captured had to be cared for and imprisoned in the early stages until the Military Police took over. They of course were also fully stretched. There were also deserters to be dealt with. If their home address happened to be on his beat a daily visit was required by the local Bobby.

He personally knew of a particular young soldier who was reported Absent Without Leave. It was a sad case. He was homosexual, which in those days was an imprisonable offence if practised. The army took a similar view. Life for the young man became unbearable and he absconded. He was the son of a friend of my father, an ex-police superintendent who had died just before the war. His widow lived in a large Victorian house which she shared with her son before his call-up.

One morning he received an anonymous telephone message informing him that a man in army uniform had been seen entering the garden shed at the rear of the house the night before. He visited the house and after courteous pleasantries were exchanged he asked his friend's widow if he could search the house as was his duty. After a brief inspection of the house he apologised for his enforced intrusion and was in the act of shaking hands with her when he noticed her eyes turn from him towards the long heavy velvet curtains covering the landing windows. Her son was standing on the sill behind the curtains. Later, when playing hide and seek at children's parties, I often copied this hiding place.

Soon after this incident it was reported that a German pilot had baled out from his stricken aircraft before it

had crashed and burnt out on the moorland. A search of the area was soon abandoned as it was very labour intensive and time consuming. There were many similar incidents. He was actually being protected and hidden by a family of sheep farmers who lived in a very remote farmhouse. They had taken pity on him and their spinster daughter, a pretty girl although rather simple, had taken a shine to him. It was several weeks before the police were informed of his presence at the farm by some ramblers who had seen him. They would have taken little notice of him except that he ran and hid when he realised he had been seen. The police immediately surrounded the farm-house but he had been forewarned of their approach and he had made his escape. After a few miles he chanced across the Manchester-Sheffield railway line and when a train stopped at the entrance of the tunnel awaiting clearance to enter he boarded an empty truck. It was a slow train stopping at several village stations and eventually he left the truck at the station halt nearest to the police house. It was cold and dark and he silently took refuge in the waiting room where he was able to warm himself on the ever-burning coke fire. Unknown to him, the station master had observed him and contacted the police house to say there was a suspicious-looking young man who was unknown to him in the waiting room. The station was otherwise deserted. Unarmed, the constable approached the waiting room cautiously, not knowing what to expect. He slowly opened the door and the frightened pilot flew at him brandishing the heavy iron poker from the fire. The fire iron struck his police helmet with a vicious blow and it was deflected, as designed to do, to his shoulder, chipping the bone. It was the worst action the German could have possibly taken. Seconds later he was writhing in agony on the waiting room floor, his left knee cap shattered by a carefully-aimed police boot. My father calmly handcuffed him and took him to the Royal Hospital. He was told to take a few days rest after seeing the police doctor. He ignored this advice and reported for duty the next evening.

'The bloody young fool. If he had come quietly I would not have found it necessary to defend myself. Now the poor sod will be a cripple for the rest of his life.'

11

Even when in his seventies, still living in the village police house, locals would often call on him for help when in trouble. Usually he would grumble – but oblige.

He was always aware of what was going on in *his* area and he would pass on any information he thought the current force should need to know. He admitted he was not much of a scholar, but he taught himself two practical skills – both he considered useful. He learned to type very effectively and took the post of area secretary for an ex-servicemen's association. This was of course voluntary and part time. He also became very proficient at sign language. This was a useful skill when taking statements from deaf and dumb people. There were a surprising number of these unfortunate mutes in his area and he was frequently called to court to assist. It also helped to identify those pretending to be mute.

His father, my grandfather, also had an interesting sideline which paid rather well. He compiled the cross-word puzzles for two Sunday newspapers – *The Sunday Sketch* and *The Herald*. It took the whole of the previous Sunday to compile the puzzles.

He had a great admiration for his colleagues in the Fire Service with whom he worked very closely during the Blitz. An old fireman friend gave him some advice. He told him always to try to avoid two major hazards whenever possible: a body and a smouldering well-peed-on mattress. The body would bring grief and masses of paperwork, the smouldering mattress would fill your lungs with a putrid stink which could take days to clear. Although this advice was passed on no doubt tongue in cheek it may have sown the seed of an idea which he was to employ at a later date.

He maintained a friendship with his old sergeant, a wise old campaigner who had fought in the Boer War and retired some years earlier. One particular hot summer's day they were having a pint together in their local, this time with the mug on the table and not under his cape, when the old man confided in him that his daughter had a problem with her neighbours. The occupant of the house next door to her was the Vice-Chancellor of a large university and was a well-known academic with political aspirations. He was frequently in the local press and on local radio and liked to mix with the city's more influential people. Theirs was a large house with extensive grounds including a tennis court. However, the only large flat lawn was adjacent to the sergeant's daughter's house. A tall hedge separated them.

The professor called on her early in the morning, which was unusual since he had not acknowledged them as neighbours during the three years they had lived there. Without any courteous pleasantries he warned her that he was holding a garden party during the afternoon and some very important guests would be attending. Some of the students graduating this year had been invited and they had also been pressed into preparing the grounds, which looked splendid. A large marquee had been erected and the college orchestra would entertain.

'There will be in excess of a hundred guests,' he informed her proudly.

His brusque message, the purpose of his visit, was, 'I don't want my guests to be looking at your washing over the hedge or listening to your baby crying all afternoon. I expect you to do something about it.'

No please or thank you – it was a command. She was very upset. She had taken advantage of the good weather to be able to do a rather larger than usual wash – curtains, etc.

Her husband, who had been invalided out of the Fire Brigade, was still not totally fit but he was always rather in awe of his famous neighbour and suggested they should bring the washing indoors until the next day.

When the ex-sergeant called in to see his grandson on the way to the pub his daughter was crying and her husband was obviously distressed. My father listened to him. He himself had been subjected to his bad manners and arrogance and had always been expected to accept it.

He put down his pint, looked thoughtful and said 'Obviously your daughter is unhappy, Sarge. Why not invite them to your house for tea. Your wife will love to see her grandson she can take him to feed the ducks. Keep them out of the way until his guests have gone home. This way everyone will be happy. By the way, Sarge, that old mattress in their potting shed, the one the dog lies on, would you miss it?'

The old man looked puzzled.

'I don't suppose so – why? Take it.'

My father mumbled something about bringing a new one for the dog, he would deliver it later. He then changed the subject.

It was a garden party to remember. The entire afternoon the neighbour and his unfortunate guests choked on clouds of acrid pee-stinking smoke. This wonderful event was brought to an early ending.

It appeared that an old mattress which had been put out for disposal had caught a spark from the dying embers of an adjacent garden fire and had been accidentally ignited. When the irate neighbour called on them for the second time in three years he was unable to get past the gate. A large well-trained guard dog menaced him and made it clear he would not be wise to enter. There was no one at home.

I suppose it could have been a coincidence!

12

We were walking slowly up the hill to the local. It was dark and the lane we had chosen this particular Friday evening was unlit. He had walked this beat many hundreds of times, sometimes on duty with his police dog, and sometimes lately with me. He pulled me to one side almost before I had noticed the headlights of a fast-moving sports car coming down the hill towards us. As the speeding car drew almost level with us a large pheasant flew across the road. It almost avoided the car but not quite. The car screeched to a halt about 20 yards behind us, then the driver slowly reversed back up

46

towards us. My father took a heavy metal torch from a pocket and hit the poor bird sharply behind the head. He then commenced to place the still-twitching body into a carrier bag he had taken from another pocket.

The young driver a little shaken said almost apologetically, 'It wasn't my fault, it flew out straight in front of me. Is it dead?'

'Yes, sir,' my father said sadly. 'I'm afraid you have killed a fine bird. Don't worry, you were within the speed limit on the correct side of the road – so no harm's done.'

The man's tone changed.

'What shall I do with it? I suppose it's mine by law?'

My father tied up the neck of the carrier bag and passed it to me.

'I'll tell you what, sir, I will have this one, you can keep the next one.'

The young driver thanked him, smiled and drove off.

13

Whenever I eat pheasant I am reminded of that incident just as I am reminded of a story of an event that he was involved with almost half a century earlier.

We were sitting enjoying a drink together and playing dominoes. He recalled that this pub had been the location of one of his more difficult cases. He would often call in for a pint and a quiet hand of dominoes (possibly the old bones we were now using) before signing on for the night shift. The locals, mostly farm workers joined by a growing number of workers from the nearby brick works, cautiously accepted his company and invited him to play with them. He would ignore some of the petty misdemeanours he overheard them discussing, but he hoped they knew where to draw the line.

One of the older members of the group never missed an opportunity to have a dig at the 'Constaberlory' as he pronounced it. He marvelled at their stupidity. He was a highly skilled very crafty poacher. My father would wear an old long gabardine raincoat over his uniform and discard it when he went on duty.

Old Pearson would say, 'You had better hurry and finish with the bones (dominoes), Bobby. It's a good moon tonight and the unofficial hunters will be out in force. They will be perfectly safe in this neck of the woods. They tell me the local lawman is too slow to catch a cold!'

He had spent many years being insulted by experts but it still annoyed him when Pearson blatantly accepted half crowns and free pints from customers – obviously as a payment for something.

'I know you are at it, Pearson, I'll get you one of these nights.'

Old Pearson grinned and said, 'Never will, Bobby. I hear you retire in about thirty years' time – you just don't have the time.'

The banter would continue thus, sometimes he even followed the alleged poacher and on two occasions had apprehended and searched him. On one occasion he found two rabbits and a ferret in the oversized pockets of the old topcoat he always wore. He was not on private land, he was not carrying a gun and there had been no complaints against him so it was hardly worth risking a court case.

One evening, a Friday when he was off duty for the weekend, he remained later in the pub than usual, since he did not need to arise early the next morning. Pearson had been drinking more than he usually did and about half an hour before closing time he slid out of a side door hoping to be unnoticed. My father had noticed him and after a few minutes he followed him. He saw him cross two fields to a copse and after about ten minutes there were two bangs from a shotgun. He waited behind a hedge next to a stile and when Pearson re-emerged from the copse and climbed the stile, he seized him.

'Got you! Let me take a look in your pockets.'

There were two pheasants and a two-piece shotgun still warm – neither being obvious from outside the coat.

'You've finally got me, Bobby, but you had to wait until I am a little worse for drink.'

He had never seen him in this state before and enquired why he had had so much this evening.

'It's my daughter's wedding tomorrow as you probably know – you seem to know everything,' he said. 'I collected these to make a pie for the reception. I have already bought two rabbits.'

He grinned sheepishly.

'I don't suppose I will be able to get to the wedding now? My wife will kill me – my daughter will never forgive me.'

He sounded so pathetic.

My parents knew and respected Mrs Pearson. She played whist with my mother and the other village ladies and she had been preparing and talking about the event for weeks. Rose, the daughter, was a trainee nurse and was also very popular and she had invited many local people.

It was a watertight case – Pearson would have to plead guilty and he would face custody. He looked down at the unfortunate man. He softened.

'Go on then, on your way and don't let me ever have need to search you again. Good luck to Rose tomorrow. I'm off duty. I'll come over to the church if that's OK with you?'

'You will be welcome, Bobby' said the now sober poacher. Thank you, sir, I won't forget your kindness. Bring the Missus to the reception, I promise I won't mention the incident if you don't.'

He awoke late on Saturday morning rather pleased with himself, and when he opened the kitchen door to pick up the newspaper – over the door handle hung two plump pheasants and a hare.

14

Some of the regulars in the pub were not indigenous to the village. They had moved in after the war. There were those who had been bombed out of their homes and were re-allocated to the temporary 'pre-fabs' which seemed to last for ever. Some married local girls and war widows and quite a few came to work in the ever-expanding brickyard – bricks were in short supply and needed more than ever for rebuilding.

The wife of one of the brickyard workers did daily cleaning for a friend of my mother. Neither of them was local so little was known of their earlier lives. Mother visited her friend for her usual Monday morning coffee and on her return told my father she was sorry for her ageing friend since her cleaner had turned up for work later than usual and although almost bed-bound she had tried to do the cleaning herself. When the woman did eventually arrive she said she did not feel well. She had a black eye and a swollen lip. She said she had fallen. Mrs Turner insisted she had a coffee with them and then return home. My mother completed the cleaning for her. Apparently this was not the first time this had happened.

My father eventually showed a flicker of interest and looked up from his *Daily Mirror*. He enquired her name. About two weeks later the cleaner sent her little daughter to Mrs Turner's to excuse her mother that day. She was unwell but she hoped to be able to come tomorrow. The little girl protested when Mrs Turner suggested that my mother should call on the cleaner and see if she could help.

The child became agitated and started to cry. She said her daddy would be very angry if anyone came to the house. Mrs Turner telephoned my mother and suggested she should make a casual visit whilst she was shopping nearby. This she agreed to do. She knocked on the door, which the little girl opened. This was sufficient for her to see the girl's mother lying on a couch – she was appalled by her state. The poor woman had obviously been badly beaten.

At this stage nothing had been reported to the police but when my mother told my father of the situation he put on his civilian jacket and went to the house. Her husband opened the door slightly and refused him entry – or even to speak to him. He recognised the man as a regular in the taproom. He was a large, good-looking but rough man who always seemed argumentative and bitter. This my father excused since he knew that he had suffered badly in the hands of the Japanese when a prisoner of war on the Burma railway. He was an intelligent man and was currently working at the brickyard as a labourer. The unfortunate man always got drunk on payday, Friday, and he took his frustrations out on his poor little wife. Uninvited, he pushed his way past Mick the labourer and insisted on seeing his wife. Mick told him in no uncertain terms that if he didn't leave his home immediately he would throw him out.

'You have no warrant and no right to interfere.'

At this moment his wife entered the room. She looked dreadful, and implored them not to awaken the children. The angry householder lunged at my father viciously and within seconds he was in the rear of the police car – handcuffed. It was a bitter cold night, it had snowed most of the day, and he drove up a lane in some tractor tracks for about four miles and ejected the shivering Mick. By this time they were about ten miles from his home.

Mick was without a coat. He removed his shirt and his shoes and told him if he ever needed to be called out again he would take him twice as far – and tell all his friends in the pub.

He decided not to charge him, this time. His wife was also too frightened to testify against him. He told him his future in no uncertain terms. The man was a coward, not just a bully, and the treatment seemed to have worked well. Mrs Turner's cleaner was a much happier lady and neither she nor my mother was ever aware of what had brought about the change in Mick.

15

My father had many admirable skills and qualities. However, he did have a weakness. He was no handyman. DIY skills were a stranger to him. He could not be trusted to put a new bulb in a torch. I once observed him in action. I watched mesmerised. He had acquired a new television set, a small square model with an oil-filled magnifying screen in front of it. There was also a primitive figure X aerial with it.

The aerial required to be fitted as high as possible and to run a co-axial cable to the set. The house is situated in a very good reception area and a friend who was knowledgeable in these matters told him it would work well in the loft.

To pass the cable from the loft to the lounge where the set was situated became a problem of mammoth proportions. The cable was not sufficiently long to go outside on the roof and down the wall, it had to be direct. He was a puzzled man. After two pints he had the beginnings of a plan, without any tools such as are required for this task, the most useful being a drill. This he did not possess.

He finally decided to make a hole in the lounge ceiling, pass the cable through it – through the airing cupboard which was directly above, through the bedroom ceiling, another hole required, and finally into the loft. I offered to collect my electric drill but he declined. I felt he thought that was almost cheating. Anyhow I did not have time, lunch was almost ready.

Mother was preparing lunch in the kitchen. I joined her and we were constantly distracted by noise and commotion from the next room. This was accompanied by the sound of heavy footsteps running up and down the stairs. After about half an hour – the noise ceased and he came to join us. He beamed proudly – his vest wet with sweat and like his face covered with thick brick dust.

'Finished,' he said. 'I think I've earned a pint.'

I went to inspect the work, fearing the worst. The cable passed from the set, through a neat hole in the ceiling. Upstairs it was the same as the cable vanished through a similar neat hole on its way to the loft. It was unbelievable. The holes lined up and there was no plaster mess anywhere.

I fitted the terminals at each end of the cable, switched on and amazingly we had a reasonable picture. He really did not have any tools – drills, bits, measure or even pliers. He had even lost his hammer.

'Go on then, tell me, how did you do it?'

Once again he beamed proudly.

'I got the poker red hot in the fire, ran upstairs with it and plunged it into the floorboard, burning a hole. I then poured water down the hole and when it appeared on the ceiling below I poked the fire-iron up into it. I repeated the operation on the next floor. If I ever need to do it again I will get a new poker, this one is not really long enough.'

At least six TV sets later the current one still uses the same aerial.

He even offered to fit me a cable in my new house if I wished. It was a kind offer. I declined.

16

I have never known a person, at least in this country, with fewer personal possessions. The usual items most of us have – watches, rings, tools – he had none. When given a penknife he would display it proudly for a day or two – and then give it away or lose it. The same with money. If he had enough for two pints, one for you and one for him, he was content. He was never sure exactly how much he earned. He would give my mother his wage packet, the type where you could see the coins through a window in the envelope, and then gratefully receive his allowance.

His only luxury was his so-called 'Detective Allowance', always a grey area in its legitimate use. He used it fully. He said it was amazing how much information you could glean for the price of a pint of beer.

His favourite shift was the two to ten stint, the afternoon he would cover the ground like a lawman in a western film – seeing and being seen by as many of the people who he always claimed 'paid his wages' – the evenings he would usually spend around the public houses in his area.

In his later years, by now promoted, he would invite me to accompany him on a tour. It was quite an experience. Everyone seemed to know him and I felt most of them even respected him – although he was always very much a policeman. As I grew older he would take me to see the results of a particularly nasty crime or to meet some despicable felon. I began to realise this was his way of putting me off the police as a career. It worked.

17

He was always very sensitive regarding the grief of others, such as relatives of victims of road accidents or when a sudden death would have to be reported to an unsuspecting relative. He hated this part of his duty and was very relieved when a new recruit came into his charge who was perfect for the task. He actually took pride in his natural gift of 'bad news breaking'. An ex-miner from Chesterfield he was a crude, uncouth, uncaring man. Often after breaking particularly bad news to some unfortunate wife or parent he would actually recount or imitate their reaction to his colleagues back at the Police Station.

His first attempt was, 'Are you the wife of Jack Wilson the bloke who keeps on trying to top himself? Well, he's managed it this time.' He said 'You should have seen his missus. She fell into a heap on the doormat.'

'Your cat's been run over by a truck. It must have been a big truck, the poor dead thing's big enough to make a hearth rug.'

'Mrs Vagen? I can now tell you, you are the Widow Vagen.'

Although he was useful he was not a popular man.

A man of predictable habits my father would return after the evening shift at 10.00 p.m. within a minute or two. One night I had finished my homework and I persuaded mother to allow me to wait up for him so that we could listen to a boxing match on the radio together. He was late.

Half past ten ... eleven o'clock ... half past eleven. By this time my mother was becoming agitated. I waited up with her. Just after midnight he came home. He looked dreadful. There was blood all over the front of his shirt and on the collar of his overcoat and he also had a nasty wound on his forehead. He said he was all right and told me to go to bed.

He put his arm around me, hugged me for a few seconds, then he said quietly, 'Don't ever be a copper, son.'

I asked him if it hurt badly. He brushed the back of his hand across his brow. Blood marked his skin.

'No it's OK, son, I've had much worse than this. It's not the cut that bothers me, it's the reason I got it that troubles me and will keep me awake tonight. There are some evil people out there.'

He looked really sad and I felt so sorry for him. I squeezed his arm and smiled at him.

'Good news, Dad, our man won the boxing.'

He said. 'Now will you go to bed? Thanks for helping your mother.'

I later learned that a six-year-old girl had been badly abused by a middle-aged man. She was able to name him, a wealthy local businessman well-known in the area. My father tracked him down. He was hiding in the local cinema. He entered the cinema halfway through the main feature film and insisted on all the lights being switched on. The cinema was very crowded and the audience were very aggrieved and abusive to him. He then located his quarry who he was hiding under the seats near the rear of the auditorium. The man was apprehended and taken back to the station to be cautioned, questioned and, hopefully, charged.

The performance continued.

There were no other officers available to assist him

with the interview and of course tape recorders were not available at this time. The interview room was a square bare room with brown lino floor covering and a plain wooden desk with a bent wood chair on either side of it.

He cautioned the man and continued to question him. After only a few minutes he admitted the offence and said that he had been led on by the six year old, describing in detail what he had done to her and surprisingly admitting how many other similar offences he had got away with.

He was well known, almost respected, locally and had no previous charges against him for anything. My father carefully wrote out the statement, read it back to him and asked him to sign it. He refused.

He said that he had changed his mind and smiling said, 'I have done nothing wrong. I admit nothing and I will see my solicitor in the morning.' He named a locally famous brief – very good, very expensive. 'I will deny I said any of the stuff you have written down – you have no one to support this pack of lies you have written.' He stood up. 'I wish to leave now. You have wasted enough of my time – goodnight.'

'You will go when I say you can' my father said harshly – he was sickened by the man's behaviour. He realised the man was playing a game with him. Of all the low-life villains he had encountered, this man represented the worst side of humanity he could imagine. 'Sit down, sir, I will continue the interview.' He looked up at the clock on the wall. 'We have all night if need be. I think you should sign the original statement.'

The man rose quickly to his feet, grasped the back of the chair he had been sitting on and swung it viciously at my father, striking him across the forehead. The paedophile was roughly overcome and put into the rear of the police car. My father was still on his own.

He had a good working relationship with his colleagues in the other services he worked with, including the medical staff at the local hospital. He lifted the unconscious man from the police car and carried him directly into the emergency department. The duty doctor he knew well and he cared for my father very sympathetically and immediately. He put fifteen very fine stitches into the wound and told him that if he would leave it alone it would heal without trace within a few days. Two of the nurses fussed over him and brought him a mug of sweet hot tea.

The next morning as he was carefully shaving he chortled and said, 'I would not have liked to have been that dirty bugger I took in last night, he yelled with every stitch. They had to sew his ear back on. It hung by a thread. I thought for a minute I had killed him. I wouldn't mind swinging for a villain like that – but not yet a while. Dr Anderson seemed to know why he had been brought in – he refused to give him anaesthetic and used the biggest needle I swear I have ever seen. You know those nurses are angels. It was worth it all for that mug of tea. I don't know how much Scotch there was in it and I am pleased to say they didn't give him any.'

Much to his disgust the man did get a good brief and the case was dropped. Fortunately he dropped his counter claim against the police for assault and the incident was forgotten – except by the child and my father.

About a month later he stood behind the same man in a queue at the wet fish shop. He had just purchased a large fresh crab which he put in his raincoat pocket.

He smirked at my father and said, 'Good day officer, I am going to the cinema – a matinee show. This time you have no reason to follow me.'

He still had a bandage over his ear.

When he emerged from the cinema about two hours later a group of around 20 local women and a few men were waiting for him. He was knocked to the ground and every one of them took retribution with him in their own particular way. There was not a policeman in sight. When they undressed him in hospital it was obvious he would never have the desire or the capability to satisfy his perversions ever again – they had made sure of that. The crab in his pocket was totally pulped – there was not an unbroken fragment of shell remaining.

Somehow the child's mother had received information naming this man as the one who had sexually abused the infant and that he had admitted it to the police. Eventually when he was well enough to leave hospital and stand trial he did admit numerous other unreported cases of the same type.

I often wonder who informed the girl's mother.

Father was friendly with the fishmonger who had sold the crab to the pervert. He would often give him a choice fillet of cod or halibut and he would take it to the fish and chip shop a few yards down the road for them to fry it for him. He saw nothing unusual about this but my mother marvelled at his cheek. No money had changed hands – it was typical of him. The owner of the chip shop had an allotment at the rear of his premises. He also had a sty with a pig they were fattening for Christmas. All the potato peelings were boiled up to feed the pig and any leftover fish from his own business and the fishmonger's was included in the swill. My father had an interest in the arrangement. He would facilitate the pig's slaughter and butchering at the right time. He also was very fond of bacon. For the entire winter after Christmas we had pork, bacon and ham all tasting strongly of fish. It was a flavour I could never get used to.

18

In later years whenever my family visited the area a certain cottage was always pointed out and remarked upon. It is the end cottage in a row next to the main road. There is a tight bend in the road and at its nearest point it almost touches the cottage. Only a drystone wall separates them. The location surrounding these mineworkers' homes has changed little except what was once the site of an open-cast coalmine is now a golf course. As we near the golf course main gateway someone always points across the road to the end window of the end cottage and remarks, 'Fat bum cottage window'. The window indicated can be reached from the top of the wall. The origin of the story was based on an incident which occurred one evening as he was patrolling his beat just after nightfall. A motorist stopped his car and informed him that there was a man trying to enter a house through the window of the cottages on the bend.

'If you hurry you will catch him.'

He quickly reached the scene to find a fat backside and legs protruding from the open window.

The inept burglar had noticed an open window and had decided to take a chance. He was firmly stuck. The house was unoccupied that evening. He tried to pull the man free. He yelled and kicked and it was impossible. Should he call the fire brigade? He tried the door and although it was locked it opened easily with one of the skeleton keys he carried. Removing the man's shoes, he

handcuffed his ankles, entered the house and pushed the man out.

He closed the window, locked the door and nicked him. This was around 70 years ago and the house has probably changed hands several times since then and I wonder if the present incumbents are aware of this historic act. My family maintain the fable.

19

As a child I always anticipated the autumn with pleasure, although somewhat tempered by the enforced return to school after the long summer holiday. Even through the war years we always spent a week in Bridlington – usually at the same boarding house.

It was necessary to take some of your own food and ration books. The landlady actually counted the slices of bread at each mealtime – one slice each adult, a half slice per child.

He was unable to borrow his beloved Morris Eight police car so we travelled by train. He needed to get permission to leave his station if longer than one night so it was a well-earned break for him. I recall beer and fish and chips were readily available. Many of the fishing boats were later laid up and some of the larger ones were at Dunkirk. *The Yorkshireman*, an ex-Humber tug from Hull used as a pleasure boat actually bore bullet hole wounds.

One year he was able to borrow a Ford Eight from my uncle who owned his own business. He also provided just sufficient petrol for the return journey. There would not be enough to enable us to journey around the area. We saved items from our own rations for many weeks and stowed them in the small boot of the Ford. These consisted mainly of eggs and egg produce from our hens.

On arriving at the boarding house he was unable to open the boot, which was self-locking. There was no key. For two days we lived off charitable contributions from fellow guests. Fortunately a man from Leeds who had lost a leg whilst serving in the Navy had a rare gift in those days. He could enter any part of a motor car using only a spoon handle. My father, a little embarrassed at his own incompetence, was amazed at the man's skills. His excuse was that he had left his skeleton keys in his uniform pocket and he did not wish to use force and risk damaging uncle's car. On our return my uncle showed us the key, it was in a leather pouch hanging beneath the dashboard.

The main event of autumn was the gathering and threshing of the wheat harvest on Thorpes Farm. A huge, noisy, frightening, steam-driven threshing machine was the highlight of the event. It was a frantic week. The machine was hired and required at the neighbouring farm the following week.

The harvesting season also heralded the arrival of the Fox family. They came to help with this annual event. They were true Romanies. I became friendly with their

two sons Arthur and George and we renewed our friendship each year.

My mother once said to me when I had misbehaved and she was cross with me, 'If you don't behave the gypsies will take you away.'

This brought a quick response from my father, he told her they were decent people and he regarded them with much more respect than some of the narrow-minded people who complained about them. Mrs Fox was a pleasant hard-working lady. I remember she dressed very colourfully and as well as helping with the harvesting she made and sold wonderful baskets made from plaited raffia. These baskets were in great demand in these years of shortages and my father persuaded her to show my mother how to make them. My mother even today still produces the occasional sample as a gift.

Mr Thorpe, the farm owner, appreciated the family's visit and he allowed them to live off the land during their stay. There was plenty of fresh water for drinking and a decent trout brook which they were grateful for. It was a good time for vegetables and rabbits were plentiful – in fact so prolific that they were a nuisance.

George, the elder son, patiently instructed me on the art of catching rabbits without the use of snares, ferrets or guns. He would collect old newspapers and pieces of rag and soak them in paraffin which he took from the lamps in their caravan. He then crept up to the warren and carefully selected a burrow in recent use. Eventually at dusk the rabbits would come out to graze. Quietly he would stuff the treated paper and rags down the hole using a long willow stick. The next step was to select and cut a long length of briar, removing all the side shoots but retaining the thorns. Rabbits hate strong smells and were fearful of the odour in their burrow. They would huddle in a group some distance down the hole.

George carefully poked the briar down the hole at about an arm's length and then twisted it slowly. Eventually he extracted it, again slowly, and hopefully there would be a terrified rabbit, its soft underbelly fur entangled with the briar. A sharp cuff behind its ears put it out of its misery. He would then repeat the operation. I learned how to do this and he made me promise only to take enough for our own table needs, just as he did.

He said, seriously, 'If you kill anything you must eat it. If you can't eat it don't kill it!'

Mr Fox had a very specific skill. He could build and repair drystone walls. It was fascinating to watch him work. He never cut a stone. He studied the shape of the stone and fitted it perfectly without the use of mortar.

His advice was, 'Somewhere there is a stone to fill the gap, and a gap awaiting the right stone, if you look hard enough.'

He passed the time when not engaged with the harvesting, building such walls all over Derbyshire.

Although he gave Mr Thorpe priority, he was always in demand by the other farmers in the area. Such walls were also becoming popular in domestic landscaped gardens and there was an obvious need and opportunity to start such a business on a more formal footing. My father suggested that he should take up permanent residence in the village and even found a derelict stone cottage which would be suitable for him to make habitable. It would enable the boys to receive regular schooling.

He said he would think about it. However, the whole family enjoyed their way of life and they looked upon this visit as their annual working holiday. Mr Fox was also a trained cordwainer. He could make and fit a pair of shoes from a sheet of hide. He made me a pair of leather sandals which were as good as new even after I outgrew them.

It annoyed my father that he was constantly receiving complaints from villagers, usually from newcomers, about the Fox family. Anything going missing – bottles of milk from doorsteps, hubcaps, dogs and cats – they always accused them. If it was an official complaint he was duty-bound to investigate and he could prove from his records that the incidents of petty theft were constant whether the Foxes were visiting or not. Often after proving their innocence, usually by apprehending the real culprit, he would demand an apology from the accuser and at the same time he would like to see their own dog, radio or car licence where applicable.

Sadly Mr Thorpe was killed when his tractor rolled on him and there was no one to continue running the farm. The stock was sold, machinery and equipment was auctioned and the farmhouse, never in good repair, quickly became derelict.

A year passed and as usual at the harvest time the Fox family arrived in their horse-drawn caravan and pitched

it in the same place as last year. Of course there was no harvest, but it was their programme so, here they were. They had been in position just two days when a man I did not recognise called at the police house. He was a very striking well-dressed gentleman – he also had a large Daimler car. He was quite rude with my father and demanded that he should evict the gypsies who were squatting on his land. It appeared that he had purchased the land and buildings some months earlier. It was his intention to develop the property. They argued rather heatedly and eventually my father said he would visit the family in the morning. He did not wish to disturb the children at this time of night.

As Mr Eaton left I heard him say he would have a word with them. However, he could not promise any immediate action as a court order would be required and this would take time, possibly weeks.

The Foxes understandably wished to stay for the usual time as planned. Mr Eaton considered the situation and

reluctantly agreed to let them stay. He warned my father that he would be in trouble if he encouraged them to either stay – or return next year. As the year passed the farmhouse was completely renovated. Mr Eaton had spent a fortune on it and gradually he extended the main building by linking it to the farm buildings, almost doubling the size of the house. It had become a very attractive ranch-style building with several more bedrooms all luxuriously fitted out.

The farmland was very extensive and the area the Foxes usually occupied was well away from the house down by the river where it was considered to be too damp for building. They were also out of sight, which explains the reason that they had been pitched for two days before Mr Eaton saw them. I had seen them and told my father.

'There will be trouble now,' he said.

Mr Eaton, as expected, revisited the police house. He sat in his car outside and hooted loudly. My father, off duty and in his shirtsleeves, met him on the garden path. Mr Eaton was furious. He castigated my father and said he was about to report him to the Chief Constable whom he played golf with and knew well. It was all my father's fault. He should have made it clear to them last year that

71

if they returned they would be trespassing. They are no longer useful. There was no harvesting for them to help with and if the police were incapable or unwilling to protect private property he would take steps himself to have them thrown out. My father reminded him that the same rules applied as before. He could not forcibly remove them, certainly not without a court order for eviction.

He allowed Mr Eaton to rant and rave and insult him for a few more minutes then he said, 'I will need to visit you tomorrow, sir. I have to serve you with a summons. It would appear you omitted to gain planning permission for the extra dwellings you have built onto the old farmhouse – they will probably have to be demolished.' Mr Eaton was aghast. He continued, 'I can tell you, sir, that at present this is not common knowledge – I don't think anyone in the village is aware of the situation.'

Mr Eaton was very unpopular, and he knew it, and it went without saying that with a little encouragement many objections to a late application for planning permission would soon appear from his neighbours.

'I suggest, sir, that a little understanding shown to this family may help your cause.'

Mr Eaton knew when he was beaten.

It was an opportune moment to have another attempt to persuade the family to take up permanent residence in the village, in a house. Once again they declined.

20

The only occasion I remember him showing any sign of stress was when he went to Nottingham to be a character witness for my grandfather who was in trouble.

Grandfather was a keen gardener and still working part-time on the railway at well past the normal retirement age. There was a local prisoner-of-war camp housing Italian soldiers and they had free access within the community during daytime, often working on farms and in the woodlands. As a child I can remember playing football with them. They were obviously very lonely, missing their families, and they would proudly show us pictures of their own children. Their part of the war was over, having fought unsuccessfully on both sides, and at this time they were almost on our side, as they would say.

My grandfather disliked and mistrusted them and although he had fought a war against the Germans and we were currently once again at war with them, he much preferred them to the 'Ities' as he called them. He considered them to be turncoats and thought it very apt that they should be made to wear a big green patch on the back of their tunics.

Food was now at its most scarce, almost everything was rationed and we were encouraged to 'dig for Victory' and take allotments. Gradually produce started to disappear from his allotment: a few eggs, a cabbage and eventually some runner beans he was growing for show. He would collect 12 pods each 26 inches long – his measure was corner to corner of the centre page of the *Daily Mirror*.

'It's those bloody Ities', he told my father. He was absolutely convinced, although he had no proof. 'I've been out several times after dark, but the cunning buggers leave it until after curfew time when they are supposed to be locked up.'

He believed that if they were caught stealing they should be shot. They had technically escaped and they were stealing our rations. My father warned him to keep his gun well hidden or he would confiscate it. My father had a telephone call from Nottingham Police warning him his father was in trouble. The officer who made the call knew my father and said he would do all he could to help – but it was serious.

Apparently more produce was being stolen each night and he decided to keep vigil one night. In the early hours of the morning a shadowy figure crept through a hole in the fence and then took cover behind a hedge he then disappeared from sight. A few moments later he crept back along the same route. This time he had a bulging canvas bag in his hand.

Suddenly he screamed in pain. His free arm was pinned to an oak tree with a garden fork. It had passed through his tunic, through the fleshy part of his upper arm and about three inches into the tree. It was impossible for him to free himself.

At daybreak my grandfather visited the local police station and informed the duty sergeant that he had captured an escaped prisoner of war (this being true) he also had proof that he had been stealing food from the enemy (again true) and he considered it to be at least a hanging offence.

He was charged with inflicting bodily harm to a person and to make the matter worse he had not reported it for over six hours. The unfortunate thief had been pinned to the tree all night. Fortunately the wound was not too severe and he made a full recovery.

People queued up to testify for my grandfather who became a local hero. Women thanked him for protecting their children from a ruthless enemy. This they certainly were not.

The judge in his wisdom bound him over to keep the peace and fined him £10. He truculently refused to pay the fine and was prepared to go to prison. However, it was promptly paid by a collection made by his grateful neighbours. He was not very contrite regarding his treatment and said he would have been awarded a medal in any other country. There were military police at the trial and he told them that they had better take this as a warning and keep the 'Ities' locked up at night and if he ever caught one of them stealing again it would be a bayonet – and not in the arm.

He then turned to my father, smiled and said, 'Thanks for coming – it was worth it to see that cowardly Itie pinned to the tree, crying like a baby.'

My father chastised him and reminded him that he now had grandchildren and should teach them by example. He said he thought he had.

He was a supporter of capital punishment and had some heated arguments with my father who was not.

His final thrust of the argument was, 'If you hang them you can be sure they will never do it again.'

21

When I started to collect material for this story it was my intention to provide a permanent record for future generations of his family – before it's too late. My mother is 96 and I am not too far from my biblical allotted span and I realise that it concerns five generations by direct contact. I have been grateful for the willing participation I have been given by family and neighbours.

My mother rummages through her filing system (it's an old shoebox) for old photographs, one of her most interesting discoveries being the front page of the *Daily Mirror* published on the day of Queen Alexandra's funeral. She explained to me that my father was on duty on The Mall and there is a very clearly recognisable image of him in Guards' uniform, his head bowed. The caption reads 'Guardsman bows his head in respect of Her Majesty as the cortege passes him.'

She claims that in fact he told her that he had lowered his head so that they could not see his lips move when he said, 'Why the bloody hell do they always choose such a cold day to snuff it?'

22

I noticed my teacher Mrs Cook walking up the path to the house. She had her dog with her and she looked angry, although I did not think I had done anything for her to complain about. She spoke to my father who after about five minutes returned, smiling.

He said, 'I always thought your teacher was a rational lady, but she must be going batty. She claims she has seen a ghost. She was serious. I listened to her politely and then advised her to come and see me if it appears again – I suppose that is the last we will see of her.'

It was only a few days later she returned. This time my father put on his tunic and drove away with her in the Morris. They drove a short distance to the ruins of an abbey, the supposed sighting of the ghost. She apparently walked around the surrounds to the ruin most evenings with her dog. She claimed now that on two occasions she had seen the apparition. A tall, thin figure in a long dark cloak. He looked like a monk. On both occasions the figure disappeared immediately on seeing her.

He instructed her to return home with the dog and he would investigate. He entered the dark ruin and gradually his eyes became accustomed to the darkness and he could also detect the smell of smoke from a wood fire. In the corner of this cell-like room he found a rough bed made from hessian sacking and the still warm embers of a fire in an old iron bucket. He settled himself as comfortably as possible and prepared for what could possibly be a long night.

He was just about to doze off when the faint sound of feet shuffling nearby alerted him. It was very eerie. The tenth-century building had a distinct creepy feel about it. A few more minutes passed and then a tall figure appeared in what had been a doorway to this cell. It was soundless and motionless. My father leapt at him and pinned him to the floor. The figure did not put up any resistance and the 16-stone policeman squashed all the breath from his body. He switched on his torch shone it in the 'ghost's' face and recognised him as the son of the family who lived in the manor house nearby. The man, now 66 years of age, had been invalided out of the army in 1915. He was a captain, a regular soldier in the Yorks and Lancs Regiment, and had been blown up in Ypres at the beginning of the war. He spent many years in a military hospital suffering from shell shock. He was a sad frightened man. Immediately this war started he went into hiding, fearful he would be re-enlisted and sent to the trenches again. Obviously his fears were groundless. Being many years over the age and unfit made him quite safe but he could not comprehend this.

Most of his relatives had passed away and his very

elderly mother was unable to help him. A place was found for him in a local nursing home where after a few weeks of regular care and food he started to recover. My father visited him on several occasions and eventually persuaded him to help with the local home guard unit. I recall seeing him walking proudly around the village in this old battle-dress tunic. He always seemed to be talking to himself out loud and I thought him very strange. My teacher was informed of the situation and she kindly helped with his recovery.

23

Old man Reilly, father of the Reilly brothers, the sheep rustlers, was a monster. Normally an affable, placid giant of a man, except sometimes on a Friday night, if he could afford the Guinness, he would drink himself out of control. His reputation went before him. Travelling boxing booths were popular just before the war in the late '30s and some of the fighters were well-known ex-professionals. Some had been title holders. A rising local star, a young heavyweight, had prospects of a great future – he was very big and very fast.

As a publicity stunt, his manager announced that he would offer three rounds with anyone who dare volunteer and award £50 if they could stay the distance. This of course would not be allowed today and was probably not legal even then. Eager challengers queued up to chance their luck. The £50 was a great temptation and the very hard steelworkers were sometimes quite confident.

Seven of them fell in quick succession until an old pro years past his best was held up by the young pretender and with a flourish the manager awarded him the money. Apparently this happened every night – the same old pro. It was all part of the act. The crowd loved it, some of the regulars started to chant, 'Reilly, Reilly, Reilly' and he was pushed over the apron rather shyly. He was sober and very alert.

The young pugilist circled him for a few seconds and then shot a lightening left to Reilly's nose. Reilly grinned and wiped the blood from his nose with the back of his glove. This had not been a heavy blow but the next one was. A long looping left caught Reilly on his cauliflower ear – it stung. Reilly narrowed his eyes and threw a right at the younger man – he was at least a foot out of range. The younger man moved in on Reilly, his intention to inflict a quick knockout. He caught him on the chin. Reilly shook his head and the young man moved in closer to finish the job. It was his first mistake. With unbelievable speed Reilly encircled him with his huge arms and lifted him bodily. He pummelled Reilly's head – to no avail. He was lifted bodily and thrown clear to the second row of the crowd.

His spirit and his shoulder broken, he looked a pathetic figure. Reilly was overcome with sympathy. He leapt into the crowd and picked him up in his arms like a baby and carried him to the dressing room. He would not accept the £50.

It was this man who two weeks later was causing trouble in the Red Lion. It was Friday night. My father, sober and several years younger, was sent to arrest him. On the last occasion this had happened it took four police officers to bring him in. They all suffered some damage.

Three of the officers held him down whilst the fourth tried to apply the handcuffs. Reilly's wrists were so thick the policemen had to jump on the handcuffs to close the handcuffs. One of the halves passed through the skin on his wrist due to his clumsy action. He was duly taken in and charged with being drunk and disorderly. It was always a dreaded call out.

On this particular night there had been a raid and several houses had been hit so the police and fire brigade were fully occupied. There was no one available to help him.

Reilly was half-sitting on a barstool leaning against the

bar. The other customers were keeping a respectful distance. Beer was rationed and they were reluctant to leave their drinks and there was the prospect of an interesting duel imminent. He was still not fully drunk and at his most dangerous and was demanding another Guinness. The terrified landlord was unable to oblige – it had all gone.

Reilly disbelieved him and said in a loud voice, 'It took four of the buggers to take me in last time. I wonder how many will turn up tonight? I know you have sent for them.' He looked ruefully at the scar on his wrist 'Somebody is going to suffer for this – I'm not so drunk tonight.'

The door opened, my father walked in.

'Just me, Paddy,' he said.

Reilly looked confused He was always respectful to my father – normally.

He walked slowly towards Reilly, who looked around for the other officers whom he expected to pounce on him.

'I told you it's just me tonight.'

He was now close enough to say something quietly into Reilly's ear. Reilly nodded and walked out briskly but unsteadily with him. The customers were nonplussed. How could one policeman scare him into submission.

The next day when asked for details of the arrest by the station sergeant he admitted he had not arrested him. He then related what had happened. He told him that a row of terrace houses had suffered a direct hit and that people were trapped in the debris. Two children who had been sheltering in the cellar were heard to be crying. It was too precarious to employ mechanical lifting gear to remove the heavy beam which had fallen over the cellar.

'Could you please help?'

Reilly lifted the beam single-handed and rescued two

little girls via a hole in the floor. It was considered too dangerous to enter the house and the policeman and Reilly were the only people allowed to try. The children were uninjured. They were the only survivors of the disaster. Seven others were not so fortunate.

They walked together towards the police car and my father said harshly to the now sober Reilly, 'Get in I need to keep an eye on you.'

Reilly protested, 'Have a heart, Bobby, are you still taking me in?'

My father smiled.

'No, of course I'm not. We are going back to the *Red Lion* – I owe you a pint.'

24

Early in 1939 war was inevitable. My father decided we must have an air-raid shelter. He and two of his brothers dug a large hole in the lawn at the rear of the house and they constructed a corrugated steel sheet Anderson shelter within the hole. It was covered with the soil they had dug out and they placed rockery stones on it. It became part of the garden landscape for many years after the war. There were two bunks, one on either side, and a short one across the rear underneath a shelf. The shelf was loaded with emergency rations: old Tizer bottles filled with water, OXO cubes, Horlicks tablets, etc. and an old spirit stone. It was an Aladdin's cave and we

children could hardly wait to try it out. When the shelter was built it was a warm dry summer, however the shelter was damp. He decided we should all have Wellington boots, his only concession to the damp. When the air-raid sirens sounded for the first time we excitedly ran down in our 'siren suits' to find our Wellington boots floating on about six inches of water. Unhappily we returned to the house and never used the shelter again.

He acquired a large sheet of steel about a half inch thick and had it cut to the exact size of the surface of the oak dining table. Covered with a tablecloth, it was undetectable. We used this as a shelter for the duration of the war. He was usually on duty during raids but when he happened to be at home and the siren sounded we would cluster under the table and he would sit on a chair next to us. We were encouraged to sing 'cheerful' songs so as not to be afraid. Obviously our parents were fully aware of the dangers. Many of our friends were killed but I have a memory of some very happy evenings spent this way. It was also exciting. We would peep out to watch the V1 and later V2 Rockets roaring with flames shooting from their motor then the pause then the explosion. The night sky would be as bright as day and burning buildings made an orange glow for hours after the raid. We would scurry back under the table, especially when the sound of shattering glass windows got nearer.

Mother would plead with him to come under the table. He always refused and said if a bomb had your number on it it will find you no matter where you hide. I was supposed to have asked him what 'my number' was.

He said, 'Don't mention your number in case Hitler hears you.'

One of the songs he tried to cheer us up with I can still recall:

> They have shifted Willie's grave to build a toilet,
> A toilet stands where Willie used to be.
> Now when I go to visit Willie
> I stand upon his grave to have a pee.

At the time I thought these songs were very daring and rude. I now realise it was his way of easing our fears.

I don't remember his discussing religion with myself or anyone else and although I attended a Church of England School and Sunday School as he expected, he considered church to be part of the social cultural world rather than the spiritual.

His father, a keen churchgoer before 'his war', came back from the trenches an atheist. When I first heard my mother whisper this word to my aunt I did not know what she meant. My father had experienced life at all levels in many countries and he was convinced that as a policeman if he needed to apprehend someone for a particularly nasty crime, he would wait to pick him up outside a church rather than outside a pub.

My first memory of the less harsh side of my grandfather's nature is an incident which occurred during a visit to his house with my father. They had arranged a men's outing to the local working men's club in order to celebrate my uncle's birthday.

My father, two of his brothers and his sister's husband

gathered for a darts tournament after watching Notts County play football. My grandfather decided to stay away from the match to care for me and then join the others afterwards. He was quite grumpy and was concentrating on compiling next week's crossword puzzle for the newspaper. He was constantly being disrupted by the twittering of his housekeeper's budgie. I was careful to be very quiet and read my comic.

It was a very old bird, ill and obviously in pain. After a bout of prolonged noisy twittering from the poor bird, he put his hand in the birdcage, grasped him by the legs and swiftly swung him, knocking his head on the edge of the table. He placed its body on the open fire and raked hot coals over it. It all happened within seconds. He took me by the hand and walked up the garden path to a small area of soft ground behind the outside toilet. He called in his garden shed and collected a trowel, a hammer and nail and two small pieces of wood. He raked up a small mound of earth with his hand trowel and placed the roughly-fashioned wooden cross he had constructed over the mound.

'Don't you say a word, young 'un, when I tell her he had died peacefully in his sleep – it will be a sad day for her. I will buy her another one on Monday. It's also a sad day for me,' he said ruefully. 'My sons and myself will be having a drink together shortly and it's a pity your Uncle John does not have the decency to join us – it may be the last chance we will have to be all together. He is the cowardly victim of a religious bigot. Your mean-minded Aunt Gladys refused to allow him to have any contact with his family – I just cannot understand her. She claims drink causes misery. I admit an excess may do, although I have never experienced this in my family. In my experience, throughout the world religion has split more families and caused more wars than beer ever did.'

At this time neither he nor I was aware of the embarrassing incident which occurred between Aunt Gladys and my father. He then poured about an inch of beer into a tall glass and filled it with lemonade.

'Drink up, young 'un, and enjoy your first beer with your grandfather.'

I did. I can still remember that wonderful first taste. When I finished the drink, he looked carefully at me.

'You'll do,' he said. 'If you say anything to her about the budgie I will tell your father that you have been drinking beer.'

25

He was a founder member of an Ex-Guardsman's Association and although the main branch was in London he was secretary of the local area in the north – mostly Derbyshire and Yorkshire.

The president of his group was a well-known duke himself an Ex-Guardsman. They often sat on the same committee. Once each year the duke would kindly invite members and their families to a garden party held on his estate. I only attended once.

My sister and myself were told to be on our best behaviour by our mother and we were dressed in our best Sunday outfits. She told us the duke was in the same regiment as our father, but of course he was a very important officer, unlike him who was just an ordinary soldier.

'He will expect you to look smart and behave well.'

My father was much less overawed by the occasion. He took me on one side and told me to be respectful to His Lordship if he should speak to me, just as I should be to any adult.

Then he looked serious and said, 'Don't show him too much respect. He is not such a good person as your mother assumes. He is married with children about your age. He has a stately home and everything you could wish for. He also has a flat in London with another woman in it. One day this will be public knowledge and I don't wish you to be too shocked when it does.'

This didn't mean much to me at the time. However,

some years later it was revealed in the national press. I still don't know how he knew or why he didn't tell mother.

He smiled and said, 'Choose your friends with care. I don't think your friend's father, Mr Fox the Romany, is so disloyal – now he is a man you can respect.'

26

Both my father and grandfather held allotments. They were similar in many ways and shared some memories.

They would carry their digging spade *en route* to the allotment on the shoulder as you would a rifle. Walking home from the allotment one lunchtime I would have been quite young as I was holding his hand and we were on the footpath which was rather busy with people walking into the village. At this time very few people owned private cars. The vicar did. He reversed quickly from his driveway which was between two high walls and

continued across the footpath. His wife was sitting beside him. They were in a hurry to get to the shops. He was a very important man in the village – we were always expected to raise our school caps to him. His car struck my leg and I fell. Although not badly hurt, I was shocked and cried out. The driver was aware of what he had done and although he slowed down he had no intention of stopping. That was until my father's spade crashed across the roof of the car causing a loud bang and an ugly dent. It would have been deafening inside the car and 'Mrs Vicar' yelled hysterically.

The angry cleric started to get out of the car using most un-vicarlike language. My father gripped him by his dog collar and hoisted him to his feet. I was still lying on the ground. He held the struggling vicar in this position and enquired of me if I was all right. I assured him I was.

He said, 'You could have killed my son with your careless driving. I remind you, sir, your role is to save souls not take them.'

The Vicar was shaken but still angry. He looked at me.

'He's not hurt. You are aware that this is my driveway. He should have been more careful, especially as he is your son, Constable.' He knew my father well, Village Bobby – Village Parson, usually there would have been mutual respect, but not any more. 'You have damaged my motor car and frightened my wife. I will report you to your superiors.'

'May I take your car registration number, sir, and I would like to see your driving licence and insurance details as soon as convenient,' was the response he got. 'I will also remind you, sir, that where a road or a driveway crosses the footpath the pedestrian has the right of way.'

He held up his arm in front of the car, holding him back. The vicar's wife was in a frightful temper but I am sure that he delayed them for what seemed an eternity, until every pedestrian in sight had passed safely.

These are minor incidents compared with some of the more dramatic events he encountered during his career. These are incidents I was actually witness to and have made a lasting impression on me.

We were returning from my grandfather's allotment this time grandfather, father and myself were anticipating a good lunch. He had managed to acquire three pork chops. As we reached the scullery door a large tabby cat leapt from the table with one of the chops between his teeth. Without speaking, grandfather swung the spade from his shoulder, neatly decapitating the cat. He bent down, took the chop from between its teeth and held it under the running tap for a minute or so, then returned it to the enamel plate alongside the other two chops

'It's all right, I will have that one,' he said.

Meat was rationed and scarce and considered too good to waste. He buried the cat then fried the chops – I cannot say that I enjoyed my lunch that day.

Outside that same scullery door there was a small York stone paved area – the backyard. One Christmas morning about a dozen men, father, grandfather, uncles and friends, were all kneeling or crouching on the surface.

One of my uncles had privileged information – he had a radio and had heard it announced that there was a strong possibility of a 'White Christmas'. All present agreed it was unlikely although the sky was glowering and heavy.

Armed with this knowledge he bet two to one there would be snow before noon. It was 11.55 a.m. and still no sign. One flake would be sufficient.

27

'He's done it now,' my father said, 'he's gone and killed Mrs Wright's cat.' The' 'he' was Rotherham Bob – or Bob, Mr Hughes's pet greyhound. Mr Hughes lived in the old manor house nearby. It was a fine seventeenth-century house with extensive grounds. Both the house and the land were in need of attention. Mr Hughes, the present incumbent, had inherited the property from his parents and although he did not have a 'proper job' he seemed to live quite well. He dabbled at most things: music, art, dog breeding and now organic vegetable production.

Bob was an ex-racing greyhound. He had been rescued from the dog's sanctuary by Mr Hughes. His distin-

guished racing career had come to an end and he was no longer earning money for his owners. Although still physically fit, he was mentally confused. He would chase cars, lorries and buses travelling up the hill next to his home. Cats were also pursued. He thought they were the electronic hares he had been taught to chase when racing.

He chased Mrs Wright's cat – caught it and killed it.

Initially Mrs Wright lodged a complaint to the police. She was very upset. However, when she cooled down and Mr Hughes offered to buy her a new kitten she withdrew the complaint. My father sensed trouble.

'This will change things now. He has tasted blood and he is not only stupid he is dangerous.'

He revisited Mr Hughes and warned him that if the dog continued to behave in this way he would have to be put down. Mr Hughes protested but he was a kindly man and he promised to keep Bob under more strict control.

It was about this time of the year when grandfather came to spend a week's holiday with my parents. As usual he spent a day at my home which was nearby. Although he was turned 80, he was still very alert and I must admit useful – especially with his help and advice in the garden. It was agreed he would stay overnight and babysit for us – he was completely trustworthy.

My son, a baby in his pram, was enjoying his afternoon sleep in the garden when suddenly grandfather rushed out of the house, grabbing an empty milk bottle on the way. He had seen Bob, standing on his hind legs reaching into the pram trying to extract milk from the rubber-teated bottle. Grandfather hurled the bottle at the dog, just missing him. The frightened dog fled to the gap in the hedge where he had entered.

The baby slept on totally unaware of the incident and there was no harm done. We were very nervous about leaving the baby unattended and we decided I should

visit Mr Hughes the next day. We had a pleasant evening and when we returned grandfather thanked us for the excellent lamb chops we had left him for his supper and the incident was forgotten.

He had washed and cleaned the frying pan thoroughly and we were impressed as to his ability for his age. I drove him to my father's house the next day and I called into the village shop to collect my newspaper.

Mr Hughes was there and he was obviously very upset. He was explaining to the shopkeeper that he must dig a deep hole to bury Bob, who had died suddenly last evening. He said his death had solved many problems since he had bitten the postman and a formal complaint was pending. Bob was well known in the area and the people in the shop generally expressed their sympathy to a tearful Mr Hughes. That was the end of that, or so I thought.

About 18 months later my father told me his father was in trouble again. He was still an enthusiastic gardener, his current specialism being large onions. A carefully prepared bed was planted out with special sets he had reared – he then tended them with loving care

97

until they were ready to show. Each one of them was over 17 inches in circumference. For three consecutive years he had been awarded the gold medal in the Railwaymen's Garden Show.

Some Hippy squatters had taken up residence in two of the allotment sheds and they allowed their dogs to run riot amongst the crops. They had caused untold damage to his almost-mature onions. He was now accused of killing two of the dogs.

My father said, 'I expect he has used his old mutton chop trick to finish them off. He should not have done it. It was not the dogs' fault. However, I doubt they will be able to prove anything against him.' My ears pricked up.

'What do you mean, his old mutton chop trick?'

I vaguely recalled his visit to my home when Bob had died.

My father said, 'I will tell you but keep it to yourself.'

He would take a kitchen sponge and cut it into segments about one and a half inches square. He then wiped the excess mutton fat from the pan, soaking up as much as possible and bound cotton tightly around the sponge, compressing it to about a quarter of its size. Three or four of these pieces were put into the freezer compartment of the fridge or if a frosty night outside on the doorstep. When the fat was set hard he would remove the cotton and throw them out into the garden in the spot most likely to be visited by dogs. Dogs love the smell and taste of mutton fat and soon gobble up the prepared sponge pieces. Within a few minutes the fat melts, the sponge expands to its normal size and the dog chokes. He could claim that he had carelessly thrown out an old cleaning sponge!

I was never sure if this is what had happened to poor Bob – I hope it was just a coincidence.

Many other allotment holders had suffered loss at the

hands of the squatters and they were very relieved when they decided to move on. An old railway pensioner who was very popular for his generosity in providing new-laid eggs from his own hens was also a victim. He prided himself on the security of his hen coop. Two large padlocks and a combination lock were fitted to the door.

The hinges he made from a piece of the thick leather straps used for the raising and lowering of railway carriage windows. One night the squatters helped themselves to all his eggs and two of his chickens. The padlocks were still in place. The thieves had simply cut through the leather hinge with a sharp blade. It was a mean theft and the old man was heartbroken. The chickens were his only bright spot in life.

My grandfather protested his innocence of the demise of the squatters' dogs. Stealing the old man's eggs did not justify such harsh revenge.

However, it proved his old addage on capital punishment, 'They don't do it again.'

In this case they never returned.

'I don't know about the Fox boys. I have just caught them scrumping Mr Parry's apples. They said they had collected them from the field behind his house. Some branches of the tree overhang the wall and some of the fruit falls outside the wall. Mr Parry has not objected so I have given the benefit of the doubt. They are bright boys who really ought to be in school with the rest of you. I will have another go at their father tonight – but I'm not hopeful.'

'Do you know the younger one still can't tell the time. He must be about eight or nine now. They always politely ask me the time when they see me. They like to look at your grandfather's old German watch. I've lent it to him. We will see if that helps him.'

My mother said, 'I suppose you can say goodbye to that. I've heard they are leaving tomorrow.'

When I went to say goodbye to them on my way to school the next morning the caravan had gone. I was sorry. I would miss them and the watch I had hoped one day would be mine. Father came in from the garden shed with a basket full of apples and the watch in his hand. You should have seen his smile.

28

A family of six children lived with their parents in what must be one of the most isolated locations in England. Their father, a gamekeeper, also tended a flock of hill sheep. They rarely had any contact with the outside world. They were very timid and they would wave shyly to passing ramblers and then scurry safely back in to the cottage.

The eldest son, John, was recruited into the army. He was the first to be exposed to the wider world. Sadly he was taken prisoner in Italy where they treated him badly. When they marched them under guard through the streets the local Italians would spit on them. The stories he returned with did little to tempt the others to leave the security of their rural safety.

After the war the army commandeered their land and cottage for use as a practice firing range. It was an ideal site, being so isolated. The whole family, much against their wishes, were rehoused in a council house in the village. This coincided with their father's retirement.

Two of the sons, Tommy and Fred, were inseparable. They had evaded any formal schooling and now as young men, although not retarded, they were backward in social skills. Inevitably they took on the role of village idiots, which to some extent they played up to and did not seem to resent.

My father was always patient with them. He would always talk to them and give them a few cigarettes and sometimes they would help him with simple tasks around the garden and allotment – especially weeding and the spreading of manure. A favourite trick the local boys would try on them would be offer a large old copper penny and a small sixpence to Tommy and ask him to choose one.

After some deliberation he would say, 'Give me the big brown one.'

This would always entertain the village boys and visitors to the village were often invited to try the trick. I mentioned this to my father and he told me that people coming out of the pub would try the trick on them.

He reminded me, 'Don't you ever tease these two brothers. They are neither stupid nor unfeeling.'

I could not understand his acceptance of them as being normal when they persistently insisted on choosing the 'wrong' coin. 'Think about it, son,' he said. 'The first time he chooses the sixpence it will be the last time he gains anything from the trick. They are very useful to me. They miss nothing that is going on. They see and understand everything.'

It was these two brothers who attracted our attention one Christmas Day lunchtime. Our family were all sitting around the dining table, aunts, uncles and cousins. We were all enjoying this traditional get-together. My cousin stood up and laughed and pointed out of the window to some movement he had observed. He was indicating some movement behind the hedge at the front of the garden. The brothers were quite short in stature and they were jumping up and down, their capped heads appearing and disappearing. They were obviously trying the attract our attention. My mother had worked hard on the dinner and she did not welcome any interference with her plans. She told my father to go out and ask them to move on. My uncle passed him a packet of cigarettes to give them with his season's greetings and my father took a plate of hot mince pies with him. He was still wearing his party hat.

I saw them refuse the gifts. They were obviously distressed about something. He returned, put on his jacket, removed his funny hat, apologised to us all and said he must go but he would return shortly. I saw him drive off with them in the police car. It was more than an hour before he returned. His dinner was spoiled, the atmosphere subdued and mother was not best pleased with him.

He told us Tommy had insisted that there was a whale in the large outdoor swimming pool nearby. Father realised that, ridiculous as it sounded, they were both so agitated and much too respectful to him to be playing a prank. He escorted them to the pool. The park where the pool was located was deserted. They pointed to the steps at the deep end of the pool where a large black semi-submerged object was trapped. It was the body of a young nun, her black habit filled with water. It did resemble a whale.

She was a nurse at a nearby military hospital staffed by nuns. She had left a note in her prayer book at the poolside begging forgiveness – she was pregnant.

29

One sunny afternoon last year my mother was sleeping on her sun lounger on the lawn behind her house. She awoke with a start. She said she felt a presence rather than hearing anything. A large figure of a man stood silently and motionless between her and the sun.

She had been orphaned and unwanted at the age of seven, had started full-time work in a lace factory at the age of 14, lived through two world wars and shared the life of a village policeman as his wife. You don't do all this without spirit. Well turned 90 and totally undaunted, assuming he was going to try to sell her something, she told him in no uncertain terms just where to go.

He spoke quietly.

'Sorry, ma'am, I didn't wish to scare you. I've come to thank you, not sell anything. Actually it's your husband I wished to thank and pay my respects to. I owe him so much However, I guess I have left it too late.

'He was instrumental in forming my adult life. He used his influence to enable me to enlist in his old regiment in the Scots Guards. I was only seventeen. I was without any qualifications and not much to offer so he must have worked hard on my behalf. I deliberately tried to follow in his footsteps.

'I spent five years as a Guardsman, ceremonial duties in London and then, unlike him, I was posted to Germany – not China. After transferring to the Military Police for two years I was demobbed. Like him, I joined the police – a special international police force was recruiting, at their base in West Germany. Fortunately, I was accepted.'

By this time my mother was fully awake and fully alert. She peered at him.

'Do I know you?'

He smiled and continued, 'I married a local girl from Dûsseldoft, had three children and now five grandchildren. It's on behalf of my eldest granddaughter that I am here.'

'I came over a few years ago, twice in quick succession for my parents' funerals – they died within two weeks of each other. I travelled here and back to Germany in the day – otherwise I would have called on you then.

'I retired at chief superintendent level over ten years ago.' He paused and looked thoughtful. 'Your husband would have been proud of me.' He smiled again. 'I outranked him. As I say, it is on behalf of my granddaughter that I am here. I don't wish to be rude but I was rather surprised to find you still living here.

'I've accompanied Heidi to Sheffield University where she has gained a place to study Social Anthropology, whatever that may be. Since my wife passed away over five years ago I have made my life around my grandchildren. I can honestly tell you they are all very familiar with my tales regarding your husband's exploits and his attitude to life in general. I must admit he was my role model. I've tried to follow his way of life as closely as possible. As I said, I've tried.'

She looked up at him and said, 'You are one of the gypsy boys.'

He replied, 'Yes, ma'am, I am George.'

Last year I visited the police house in order to sketch the building. I was standing on the footpath outside the house, when a little old lady tapped me on the shoulder. I vaguely recognised her. She said, 'You know young man, there once was a Bobby lived here'. Hence the title.